# A PROPER TEA

In memory of
Edith Mary Heap,
my grandmother, who
gave me my first cup of tea.

Grace —
now when you come
over to America, I'll
be able to have a "Proper Tea"
for you! Best Wishes..
Janice Segur
1989

# A Proper Tea

Devised and Illustrated by Joanna Isles

PIATKUS

This edition first published in
Great Britain in 1987 by
Judy Piatkus (Publishers) Ltd of
5 Windmill Street, London W1

Produced by Johnson Editions Ltd
15 Grafton Square, London SW4 0DQ
Text: Frances Bingham
Editor: Gabrielle Townsend
Art Editor: Lorraine Johnson
Cookery adviser: Penny Clarke
Artwork production: Danny Robins

British Library Cataloguing in Publication Data
A Proper Tea: an English collection of recipes and anecdotes.
1.   Tea —— Social aspects —— Great Britain
I. Isles, Joanna
394.1'2      GT2967.G7

ISBN 0-86188-668-2

Typeset by Fowler Printing Services, London
Printed and bound in The Netherlands by Royal Smeets Offset, Weert
Colour separation by Fotographics, London/Hong Kong

Our grandmother sliced slivers of buttered white bread horizontally from a cottage loaf. The wholesome aroma of a cake almost baked wafted from the Rayburn. It was one of those rare days when the sun might just stay out till evening. For the first time that year the double doors were open to the garden, bright with pinks and nasturtiums. Grandfather brought out the table covered with a beautifully laundered cloth he had embroidered himself. I, unaware at such a young age of how great a responsibility I had been given, carried out the Crown Derby tea set. Silver sparkled in the sunlight: teaspoons chinking as my brothers laid them in each saucer; a polished dish holding glistening homemade bilberry jam; and the teapot, borne by Grannie, together with the rest of the feast.

Along with many other families that bee-buzzing, rose-scented afternoon, we were about to enjoy the occasion of tea. From the lazy days of strawberry picnics to the toe-toasting warmth of a fireside cuppa, with Grandfather quietly snoozing on the rug, this book has been created from those nostalgic teatimes. I hope it may inspire many more such happy occasions.

# CONTENTS

'Tea leaves come in a thousand different shapes: some look like the boots of a Tartar, some like the breast of a buffalo, some like clouds approaching from the mountains; some look like the rippling on the water caused by a breeze, some have a dull brown colour and look like freshly ploughed soil covered with puddles after heavy rainfall. All these are good teas.'

From *An Ode to Tea*, AD 780, by Lu Yu

Tea comes from the plant *Camellia sinensis*, a hardy evergreen shrub. It grows in warm and humid sub-tropical climates, and at higher altitudes in the tropics. Besides China, its country of origin, tea is also grown today in India, Bangladesh, Sri Lanka, Indonesia, Taiwan, Japan, Turkey, Kenya, Malawi and other African countries, the USSR and Argentina.

In cultivation, tea plants are kept pruned to bush size to make picking easier – wild tea plants can grow to trees 30ft high and traditionally the Chinese used monkeys to help them collect the leaves. Harvesting consists of plucking the new shoots from the bush when the first two leaves and a bud have formed. Picking can take place throughout the year, although the best tea is that picked in April and May, the 'first flush' of shoots of the new season. Tea is then sorted and graded according to appearance into Broken and Leaf teas, each category being sub-divided into three grades: Orange Pekoe, Pekoe and Pekoe Souchong.

The leaves can be treated in various ways to produce different types of tea. For green tea, the leaves are steamed, then, while still damp, rolled and fired; for black tea, the leaves are first laid out to dry and wither, then rolled and fermented, a process which makes the leaves turn to their familiar coppery-brown colour and also imparts a robust flavour. A third type, Oolong, which has a flavour something between the two, goes through a similar process to black tea but is fermented for only a very short time.

There could be as many different teas as there are wines, for soil, altitude and climate influence the final flavour of the tea as much as the processing it undergoes. No two vintages are quite the same; thus teas are blended not only to produce special flavours but also to ensure consistent quality and flavour in each named brand.

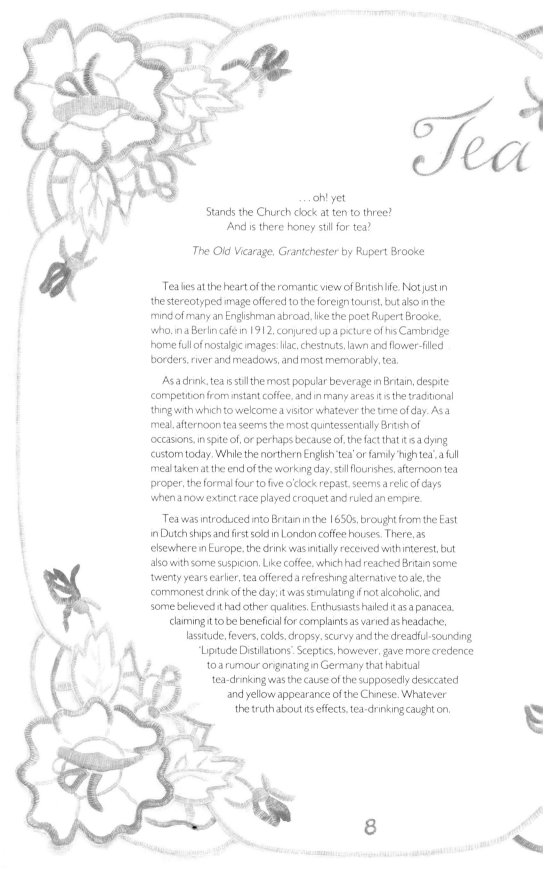

*Tea*

...oh! yet
Stands the Church clock at ten to three?
And is there honey still for tea?

*The Old Vicarage, Grantchester* by Rupert Brooke

Tea lies at the heart of the romantic view of British life. Not just in the stereotyped image offered to the foreign tourist, but also in the mind of many an Englishman abroad, like the poet Rupert Brooke, who, in a Berlin café in 1912, conjured up a picture of his Cambridge home full of nostalgic images: lilac, chestnuts, lawn and flower-filled borders, river and meadows, and most memorably, tea.

As a drink, tea is still the most popular beverage in Britain, despite competition from instant coffee, and in many areas it is the traditional thing with which to welcome a visitor whatever the time of day. As a meal, afternoon tea seems the most quintessentially British of occasions, in spite of, or perhaps because of, the fact that it is a dying custom today. While the northern English 'tea' or family 'high tea', a full meal taken at the end of the working day, still flourishes, afternoon tea proper, the formal four to five o'clock repast, seems a relic of days when a now extinct race played croquet and ruled an empire.

Tea was introduced into Britain in the 1650s, brought from the East in Dutch ships and first sold in London coffee houses. There, as elsewhere in Europe, the drink was initially received with interest, but also with some suspicion. Like coffee, which had reached Britain some twenty years earlier, tea offered a refreshing alternative to ale, the commonest drink of the day; it was stimulating if not alcoholic, and some believed it had other qualities. Enthusiasts hailed it as a panacea, claiming it to be beneficial for complaints as varied as headache, lassitude, fevers, colds, dropsy, scurvy and the dreadful-sounding 'Lipitude Distillations'. Sceptics, however, gave more credence to a rumour originating in Germany that habitual tea-drinking was the cause of the supposedly desiccated and yellow appearance of the Chinese. Whatever the truth about its effects, tea-drinking caught on.

8

# Time

At court in the 1660s, tea was made popular by Charles II's queen, Catherine of Braganza, who brought it from her native Portugal, a country which then had a thriving trade with the Far East. Though at first a fashionable luxury, as the tea trade expanded it grew progressively cheaper and eventually became the common drink for the entire nation, rich and poor alike.

In the town houses and stately country homes of the rich, tea, and its rival, coffee, became the thing to drink after meals. It was in this setting that the rite which we know today as afternoon tea began to evolve. Tea and coffee were brewed up by the hostess herself after dinner and supper, and sometimes the women would retire to the drawing room to enjoy these hot drinks while the men stayed at the table with their port. The dramatist William Congreve, writing in the 1690s, said it was 'tea and scandal' that the women retired to after dinner. So even in those early days of tea-drinking the beverage had become associated, in the minds of men at least, with feminine gossip.

It was not until the nineteenth century that the women of the British middle and upper classes perfected their way of taking tea. As social habits changed, meal times gradually shifted. While in the late eighteenth century breakfast was taken around 9.30, dinner (the main meal) at 4 or 5, and a light supper at 10, in the early nineteenth century dinner was moved to 6.30 or 7. Luncheon was introduced, supper began to disappear, and as dinner grew progressively later the gap in the afternoon between meals lengthened. It was the Duchess of Bedford who is said to have had the bright idea of filling the gap with tea and cakes, inviting friends to her boudoir around 5 o'clock and offering them a delicate meal to quell the pangs of hunger!

By the 1850s, the meal had been transferred to the drawing room; it became the focus for social visits, and the housekeeper in a grand house had the daily task of arranging the preparation of a tremendous variety of cakes, biscuits and preserves for the occasion. Afternoon tea became an institution: a pattern was laid down, in menu and manners, so firmly that more than a century later afternoon tea still gives us a taste of Victorian England.

The ships that brought tea from China in the seventeenth century brought also the implements for making and drinking it in the Chinese style, often packed, together with lengths of silk, in the hold beneath the tea chests. In the three hundred years since then the British have developed their own way of drinking tea and an array of dishes and vessels to go with it. In 1660, when Samuel Pepys recorded drinking his first cup of tea, he probably drank either from a handleless bowl like those the Chinese use today, or from the accompanying deep-sided, flat-bottomed saucer – in those days tea was often served in a cup then poured into the saucer to cool and drunk directly from it. More than a century was to pass before the creation of the cup and saucer as we know them now, with a handle on the cup and a circular indentation on the bottom of the saucer. Other items – cream and milk jugs, sugar, slop and spoon bowls, caddy, teapoy (small three-legged table) and silver tea kettle, dishes, plates, teaspoons and mote-spoons in addition to the basic teapot, cups and saucers – came into use over the next two hundred years to make up the full equipage of Victorian and Edwardian tea parties.

Ceramic tea sets were not made in Britain until the mid-eighteenth century. Thomas Whieldon and Josiah Wedgwood became known for their salt-glazed stoneware; most striking were moulded teapots – some in cauliflower and pineapple shapes – glazed in strong yellows and greens or in distinctive marble and agate effects. Other factories such as those at Chelsea, Bow, Bristol, Derby and Worcester made fine tea sets of soft-paste porcelain.

Chelsea ware was particularly highly regarded, and King George III and Queen Charlotte are known to have spent £1,200 on Chelsea tea and coffee sets as a gift to the Queen's brother-in-law, the Duke of Mecklenburg-Strelitz. (Clearly, Queen Charlotte was a keen supporter of the industry; she also bought Wedgwood's simple, cream-coloured stoneware which was then dubbed Queensware.) Neither the stoneware nor the soft-paste porcelain could equal the heat-resistant qualities of Chinese hard-paste

porcelain, however; it was only in the 1790s that Josiah Spode in Staffordshire developed bone china, a British porcelain that could truly rival the Chinese.

The inspiration for early British designs was clearly oriental. Even Georgian delftware, inspired by the continental stoneware, used blue-and-white chinoiserie motifs alongside characteristically Dutch windmills and landscapes. Chinoiserie, indivisible from tea-drinking in our minds, often reasserted itself in later years, most notably in the Willow Pattern and other Staffordshire blue-and-white ware, and in the Mikado-like designs of the Japan craze of the 1860s. An equal number of designs, however, have been purely European in inspiration, working from traditional motifs or reflecting the art movements of the day: neo-classical, rococo, art nouveau, art deco. The shapes of teapots have been as varied as the decoration: round, oval, hexagonal, boat-shaped, tall and straight-sided, short and bulbous. Every now and then there is a fad for more fantastical teapots in the shape of human figures, houses, animals and other unlikely objects. Thought tempting, it would be a mistake to regard these as new-fangled, European kitsch: even the classic Chinese Yi-Hsing pots have gone through strange metamorphoses as temples, joky figures and mythical beasts.

THE NANKING CARGO

On January 3 1752 a merchant ship of the Dutch East India Company, the *Geldermalsen*, sank in the South China Sea en route from Canton to Holland. It was found in 1985 with much of its cargo of 'Nanking' china (a generic term given particularly to blue-and-white porcelain in the eighteenth century) preserved in perfect condition. This design, 'Batavian Bamboo and Peony', is an example of a teacup and saucer mass-produced for the export market.

## How To Make Tea

Fill the kettle with fresh water from the cold tap
and set to boil. When the water is nearly boiling, pour a little
into the teapot, swill it around to warm the pot, then pour it away
and add the tea leaves. As to the quantity of tea, the old adage 'one spoonful
for each person and one for the pot' does not always hold true: treat it as no more
than a rough guideline to be modified according to personal taste, the size of the pot and
the strength of the tea leaves. Take the pot to the kettle and the moment the kettle
starts boiling hard, pour the water on to the tea leaves. Put the lid on and leave
the tea to steep for 3-5 minutes. If necessary, the pot may be topped up
later with more boiling water. And though a cosy will keep it hot
longer, remember that it will also cause
the tea to 'stew'.

## A Chinese Way To Make Tea

'Take water from a running stream and boil it over a lively fire;
that from the springs in the hills is best and river water the next, while well
water is the worst. A lively fire is a clear and bright charcoal fire. When making an
infusion, do not boil the water too hastily, as first it begins to sparkle like crabs' eyes,
then somewhat like fishes' eyes, and lastly it boils up like pearls innumerable,
springing and waving about.'

From *Brewing Tea in the Examination Room*
by Su Tung-p'o (1036-1101)

# TYPES OF TEA

Tea, like wine, should be carefully chosen to accompany the food it is served with. The following types of tea have been selected to complement the tea menus in this book. There are notes on the special character of each tea and on how to serve them.

### DARJEELING

From the foothills of the Himalayas, a fine tea with a good colour and delicate 'muscatel' flavour. Known as the 'champagne' of teas, Darjeeling served with milk or lemon, would be appropriate for *A Proper Tea*.

### BLACKCURRANT TEA

An unconventional blend of selected oriental teas enhanced with the fragrant aroma and delicious flavour of blackcurrant. Serve it without milk, hot or iced, as a treat for *A Nursery Tea*.

### LAPSANG SOUCHONG

From the province of Fujian in south China, a large-leaf tea with a distinctive smoky or tarry flavour derived from the soil in which it is grown. It can be drunk with or without milk, or iced with lemon, and is refreshing on a hot afternoon for *Tea in the Garden*.

### EARL GREY

A traditional blend of China and Darjeeling teas, scented with oil of bergamot. It was created by the Chinese for the second Earl Grey. Serve it with or without milk, or order it when you go *Out to Tea*.

### YUNNAN

A clear, golden China tea from the south-western province where the tea plant was first grown. Drink it black or with a little milk for *Tea by the Fire*.

### CEYLON

A smooth, golden tea with a delicious bouquet, made from broken orange pekoe leaves grown in the hills of Sri Lanka. It tastes good with milk, delicious with lemon or iced, and would be ideal for *Tea on the Verandah*.

### ASSAM

A strong, bright-coloured tea with a malty flavour, blended from leaves grown in the Brahmaputra valley in Assam, northern India. Drink it with milk at a hearty *Farmhouse Tea*.

### CHINA OOLONG

A unique large-leaf tea with a delicate flavour likened to 'ripe peaches'. Best served black or perhaps with a slice of lemon, this sophisticated tea would be appropriate for a *Tea Dance*.

### ROSE POUCHONG

China tea from Guandong province, mixed in the traditional way with rose petals to give a fragrant liquor. Serve it black or with just a drop of milk for *A Bizarre Tea*.

### RUSSIAN CARAVAN

A blend of fine quality China and Taiwan oolong teas, delicious with or without milk, hot or iced. It was traditionally brought across Asia to Russia by camel caravan, and might now be taken on *A Picnic Tea*.

### GREEN GUNPOWDER

The traditional Chinese green tea, with leaves curled into grey-green pellets that resemble lead shot. Made a little weaker than Indian teas, the delicate, straw-coloured liquor should be drunk by itself. Its explosive associations might make it suitable for *A Tea Party*.

### KEEMUN

A traditional black China tea with a light, delicate flavour, from Anhui Province. It can be drunk with or without milk, and goes well with Chinese food. Try it for *A Black and White Tea*.

### ENGLISH BREAKFAST

A traditional blend of Ceylon and Indian teas which gives a full-bodied liquor. This sprightly tea, taken with milk or lemon, makes the perfect early-morning 'cuppa' for *Tea in Bed*.

# A Proper Tea

*'I believe it is customary in good society to take
some light refreshment at five o'clock',*
says *Algernon in Oscar Wilde's play*
The Importance of Being Earnest, *referring to
the tea laid out to impress his Aunt Augusta.*

The menu offered by Algernon in Wilde's 1895 play would still be just the thing to prepare for a visiting aunt: finely sliced bread-and-butter and wafer-thin cucumber sandwiches, followed by cake. This is the basis of the classic afternoon tea of Victorian and Edwardian England. In this leisured world, servants daily set up a folding tea-table in the drawing room or spacious hall of a country house, or in the garden in summer, spread on it a linen tablecloth, and laid out the china and the tea tray. The teapot, slop bowl, sugar bowl and milk jug, cups and saucers were placed on one table by the hostess's chair, plus a silver tea-kettle with a spirit lamp underneath. Side plates, knives, and all the food were then laid out on another table within easy reach of the guests. No servants were required at the meal as the hostess herself, with studied informality, made and poured the tea. The male guests would hand round the cups and pass sandwiches or biscuits.

Triangles of bread-and-butter and sandwiches were arranged on large plates, with cakes and light biscuits perhaps on a separate cake-stand; hot scones, buttered or anchovy toast, buns or crumpets, might also be provided, kept warm in a silver chafing dish or beside the fire. Both China and Indian tea were usually on offer, the Indian tea optionally taken with milk and sugar, the China most properly taken by itself or with a slice of lemon.

A modern afternoon tea need not require so much paraphernalia. A fine tablecloth, pretty china and a few dishes will suffice. For the real properness of a tea lies not in the elegance of the implements nor even in the delicacy of the food, but in the way in which it is conducted. The appropriately inconsequential conversation of the guests will be punctuated by the time-honoured questions of the hostess: 'China or Indian?... Milk and sugar?... One lump or two?'

## Plain Bread and Butter

white or brown bread
butter

Cut thin slices of bread, using a really sharp carving knife if you do
not have a good bread knife. Beat the butter in a bowl to ensure it is very soft
and will spread easily. Spread the butter on the slices of bread, trim off the
crusts and cut into fingers or triangles.

*NB* Bread and butter as thin as this should not be cut too far in advance. If it
has to be cut an hour or so ahead, arrange it on the plate on which it will be
served, wrap in cling-film (plastic wrap) and put in the refrigerator.

## Cucumber Sandwiches

1 cucumber, peeled and thinly sliced
white wine vinegar
day-old brown or white bread, thinly sliced
butter, softened
parsley sprigs

Lay cucumber slices on a plate and sprinkle with vinegar. Cover and put on
one side for 30 minutes. Then drain in a sieve or colander to remove the
excess liquid. Butter the slices of bread. Cover a slice of bread with slices of
the drained cucumber, top with another slice of bread and press firmly
together. Cut off the crusts and cut each sandwich into triangles or fingers.
Arrange on a serving plate and garnish with sprigs of parsley.

### ELEGANT SUGAR THINS

8 oz/225 g butter
8 oz/225 g caster (superfine) sugar
1 egg, beaten
1 tbsp/15 ml double (heavy) cream
10 oz/285 g plain flour, sifted

½ tsp/2.5 ml salt
1 tsp/5 ml baking powder
flavouring: vanilla essence or
    lemon juice or ground ginger
extra caster (superfine) sugar

Cream the butter and sugar, then add the egg, cream, flour, baking powder and salt. Divide the dough into three and flavour each piece differently. Form the dough into long rolls about 2 in/5 cm in diameter and wrap each one in foil. Put in the refrigerator overnight. Preheat the oven to Gas 5/375°/190°C. Take dough from refrigerator and cut off very thin slices. Place on baking tray and sprinkle with sugar. Bake for about 5 minutes – they should be pale golden. Cool on a wire rack.

*NB* The dough keeps well, so any that is not used can be rewrapped and replaced in the refrigerator.

## Chocolate Brandy Cake

5 eggs, separated
7 oz/200 g caster (superfine) sugar
4 tbsp/60 ml plain
   (unsweetened) chocolate, grated
2 tsp/10 ml ground cinnamon
pinch ground cloves
1 lemon, finely grated rind and juice
3½ oz/100 g ground almonds
4 tbsp/60 ml brandy

4 oz/125 g dried breadcrumbs
1 heaped tsp/7 ml baking powder
10 fl oz/284 ml double (heavy)
   cream, whipped
5 oz/140 g plain (unsweetened)
   chocolate, grated
chocolate leaves, made from
   8 oz/225 g plain (unsweetened)
   chocolate, melted

Preheat the oven to Gas 3/325°F/170°C. Beat the egg yolks and sugar together until light and creamy. Stir in 4 tbsp/60 ml grated chocolate, cinnamon, cloves, lemon rind and juice, ground almonds and brandy, Whisk the egg whites until stiff, then fold into the chocolate mixture. Mix the breadcrumbs and baking powder and fold into the mixture. Turn into a greased 9 in/23 cm loose-bottomed cake tin and bake for 65 to 70 minutes, or until a skewer inserted into the centre comes out clean. Turn on to a wire rack to cool. When cool spread the top and sides thinly with the cream. Press grated chocolate over the sides, pipe remaining cream on the top and decorate with chocolate leaves.

*Chocolate leaves*

Melt the chocolate in a double boiler, or in a basin in a saucepan, over barely simmering water. Stir the chocolate until smooth and thin enough to spread evenly and easily. Select leaves with a rather leathery surface, such as rose leaves, as they are easier to handle. Wash well and dry. With a fine ½ in/1 cm pastry brush, brush the shiny side of a leaf with the melted chocolate, working quickly and with as few brush strokes as possible. Make sure no chocolate goes over the edge of the leaf, otherwise the chocolate will not come away cleanly. Place chocolate-covered leaves on a baking sheet lined with non-stick baking paper and refrigerate until hard. Gently peel the leaf away from the chocolate, and return the chocolate leaves to the refrigerator until needed.

For generations of British children, up until the 1930s, the nursery was a special domain. It had its own order, its own customs, foods and entertainments, and its own inhabitants: children firstly, then nurse or nanny – or governess when the children were old enough to take lessons and the nursery had become the schoolroom as well. Other adults appeared there only as exotic visitors from the great world downstairs.

Tea in the nursery could be the most enjoyable of meals. It was relatively free of the strictures of the dining-room, where children had to be quiet and well-behaved, use their knives and forks correctly and eat up everything they were told was good for them. At nursery tea, the table was simply cleared of games or lessons and covered with a tablecloth, then nanny poured the tea while the children gathered round to eat bread and jam, hot toast, delicious sandwiches, buns, muffins and cakes. Or so we might imagine from the wonderful children's tea recipes that have been handed down to us. In fact, the sweetest and tastiest foods were generally reserved for special occasions.

A child of the 1890s, Gwen Raverat, one of Charles Darwin's grand-daughters, recorded in her memoirs, 'There was only bread-and-butter and milk for tea, as jam might have weakened our moral fibre; and sponge cakes when visitors came.' This strict regime was only gradually relaxed. A typical nursery tea twenty years later, as recalled by a child of the time, consisted of, first, bread and butter, then more bread cut from the loaf and spread with jam alone, and finally, cakes, which were usually 'of various plain varieties including those flavoured with the hated caraway seed'. When Alice had tea with the Mad Hatter, all she got was a cup of tea and a slice of plain bread and butter. In nurseries all over Britain, how many young readers must have sympathized with her!

## Banana Sandwiches

bananas, halved and thinly sliced lengthways
brown bread and butter, sliced thinly
lemon juice
brown sugar
nuts, finely chopped

Put a layer of banana slices on a slice of the brown bread and butter. Squeeze a little lemon juice over them, sprinkle with some brown sugar and a few nuts. Top with another slice of bread and butter, press together, trim off crusts and cut into triangles.

## Cinnamon Toast

white bread, thinly sliced
2 eggs
½ tsp/2.5 ml salt
½ pt/284 ml milk
few drops vanilla essence
2 oz/60g butter or margarine
cinnamon
caster (superfine) sugar

Cut the crusts off the bread and cut each slice into three fingers. Beat the eggs with the salt and milk until smooth. Flavour with a few drops of vanilla essence. Dip the bread fingers into the mixture. Heat the fat in a heavy frying pan, add the fingers of bread and fry on both sides until crisp and golden. Drain on kitchen paper and dust lightly with cinnamon and sugar. Serve immediately.

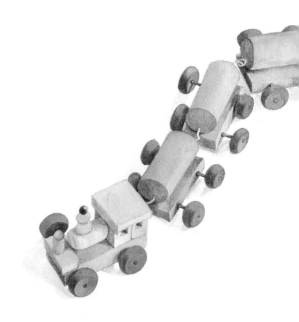

## GOD'S KITCHELS
*(makes about 12)*

1 lb/455 g puff pastry
2 oz/60 g butter or margarine
8 oz/225 g currants
3 oz/90 g candied peel, chopped
2 oz/60 g ground almonds
1/2 tsp/2.5 ml ground cinnamon
1/2 tsp/2.5 ml ground nutmeg
caster (superfine) sugar

Preheat the oven to Gas 7/425°F/220°C. Roll the pastry out to about 12 in/ 30 cm long and 6 in/15 cm wide, then cut in half. Melt the butter, add the currants, peel, almonds and spices and mix well. Put half the pastry on to a baking sheet, and cover with the fruit and spice mixture, leaving a space all round the edge of the pastry. Dampen this strip with water, place the other piece of pastry on top and press it gently down, pinching the edges firmly together. With the back of a knife mark the top into divisions about 2 in/5cm square but do not cut right through. Bake the cake for about 25 to 30 minutes, until risen and golden. When cooked, remove from oven, sprinkle with caster sugar and return to the oven for a few minutes for the sugar to melt. Cool on a wire rack and cut into separate squares before quite cold.

## Swiss Roll Roadster

3 eggs
3 oz/75 g caster (superfine) sugar
3 oz/75 g plain flour
extra caster (superfine) sugar
raspberry jam

Preheat the oven to Gas 6/400°F/200°C. Line and grease an 8 × 12in/ 20 × 30 cm Swiss roll (jelly roll) tin.

Whisk the eggs and sugar together in a large bowl until the whisk leaves a trail on the mixture's surface, then gently fold in the flour. Turn the mixture into the prepared tin and smooth the surface. Bake for 10 to 12 minutes, or until pale golden and springy to the touch. Sprinkle a sheet of greaseproof paper with sugar and place on a slightly damp, clean cloth. Turn the sponge out on to the sugared paper and remove the lining paper. Spread the sponge generously with jam and carefully roll up from one of the short ends, using the cloth to help. Trim the ends. Put on a wire rack to cool.

*NB* The crumbs from the trimmings can be used in other recipes, for example rum truffles. Some of the many varieties of Maids of Honour (page 39) use cake crumbs instead of bread crumbs.

### Icing (frosting) and decoration

4 oz/125 g icing (confectioners') sugar
lemon juice and yellow colouring to mix
fruit for decoration: orange and apple slices, grapes, blackberries

Mix icing sugar with lemon juice and yellow colouring to a thick consistency. Cover top and sides of Swiss roll. Before icing sets, decorate with fruit to look like a car, as in the illustration. This should be done shortly before serving as the juice from the fruit may run and spoil icing.

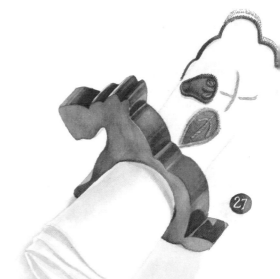

The Chinese were the first to enjoy tea in the garden. More than a thousand years ago, the cultured mandarins of Soochow and Hangchow sipped tea from fine porcelain cups while they contemplated an elegantly contrived view from a tea house set among lotus-filled lakes, grottoes and rustic bridges. The Japanese elevated such tea-taking into an art. And the English, in a less intellectual, thoroughly occidental way, have also cultivated the pleasure of tea in the open air.

In the late eighteenth and early nineteenth centuries, Londoners flocked to the famous Tea Gardens in the countryside at the city's edge, in places such as Marylebone, Bayswater, Chelsea, Vauxhall, Lambeth, Hampstead and Bermondsey – all long since absorbed into urban sprawl. The Gardens offered some spectacular attractions: many had concerts, firework displays and illuminations; some offered sports such as bowls or skittles, cricket and the old game of fives (somewhat similar to squash); others, such as Sadler's Wells, possessed mineral springs. In every garden, however, summer afternoons and evenings were spent promenading and drinking tea at refreshment tables in leafy arbours or pavilions. The gardens were open to all – men and women of all classes – for three or four days a week from April or May to September. All, that is, who could afford the small entrance fee of one shilling, or two shillings and sixpence (tea and bread-and-butter included) for the select Ranelagh Gardens in Chelsea.

In private houses, when the custom of afternoon tea was established, it became usual to take it in the garden in summer. In a cottage garden, a tray might be carried out to a simple table beneath an apple tree, while in grander households a tea-table might be formally laid on the terrace or beneath a Lebanon cedar. Tea was savoured as the shadows lengthened on green lawns, turning these leisurely moments of late afternoon into, as Henry James described it, 'an eternity of pleasure'.

## NORWICH COQUILLES
*(makes 20)*

2 oz/60 g caster (superfine) sugar
1 oz/30 g fresh yeast (or half quantity of dried)
½ pt/284 ml warm water
1 lb/455 g plain strong bread flour
2 oz/60 g butter
1 egg, beaten
½ tsp/2.5 ml salt

Cream the yeast with the sugar and stir in the water. Rub the butter into the flour with the fingertips, then add the egg and salt. When the yeast liquid has a froth on top, mix in the flour and knead the resulting dough well. Leave in a warm place to rise. When the dough has doubled in size, knock it down and divide into 20 pieces. Roll each piece into a smooth ball and put it in a greased and floured scallop shell (or shell-patterned bun tins) and slightly flatten the top. Leave the balls of dough to prove while the oven heats up to Gas 6/400°F/200°C. Bake for 20 minutes, or until golden. Turn out and cool on a wire rack. When serving, arrange patterned sides uppermost.

## Strawberry Shortcake

8 oz/ 225 g plain flour
2 tsp/ 10 ml baking powder
pinch salt
4 oz/ 125 g butter or margarine
a little milk
1 lb/455 g strawberries
4 oz/125 g caster (superfine) sugar

Grease two shallow round cake tins 7 to 8 in/18 to 20 cm in diameter and line the base of each with a disc of greased greaseproof paper. Preheat the oven to Gas 7/425°F/220°C. Sieve together the flour, baking powder and salt, and rub in the butter or margarine until the mixture resembles coarse breadcrumbs. Gradually add enough milk to give the mixture the consistency of soft dough, stirring the milk in with the round-ended blade of a knife. Turn the dough on to a floured board or working-surface, divide in two and press each half into a prepared cake tin and bake for 15 minutes. Meanwhile prepare the filling. Hull and wash the strawberries. Put some aside for decorating the top of the cake, mash the rest with a fork and stir in the caster sugar. Leave until the sugar has dissolved. When the shortcake has baked, remove from the oven and tins and put on a wire rack to cool. When cold spread half the filling on one cake, place the second on top and cover with the rest of the filling. Decorate the top with the whole strawberries.

## Quince and Geranium Jelly

5 lb/2.3 kg quinces or japonica quinces
water
1 lb/455 g granulated or preserving sugar to every 1 pt/568 ml juice
3-4 lemon-scented geranium leaves

   Wash quinces, removing any bad parts and chop. Put in a preserving pan
with enough water just to cover them. Bring to the boil, reduce the heat and
simmer for 25 minutes until soft and pulpy. As the fruit softens, mash it
occasionally to help the juices run. Pour fruit and juice into a clean jelly bag, or
strain through a muslin cloth lining a colander or other type of sieve, and leave
to drip into a large bowl overnight. Do not squeeze the bag or it will make the
jelly cloudy. Measure the juice and pour into a pan with the correct amount of
sugar. Heat very gently, stirring occasionally, until the sugar has dissolved.
When it is completely dissolved raise the heat and bring to the boil. Add the
leaves, tied together, and boil for 10 minutes, or until setting point is reached.
Remove the leaves and pour the jelly into clean, warm, dry jars. When cool
cover with wax discs and seal. Label and store in a cool dry place.

## Tea Ice Cream

1 pt/568 ml milk
1 in/2.5 cm vanilla pod
2 level tbsp/30 ml dry tea
4 eggs, beaten
6 oz/170 g caster (superfine) sugar
½ pt/284 ml double (heavy) cream

   Bring the milk, with the vanilla pod in it, to the boil, pour over the tea and
allow to brew for 5 minutes, then strain off the liquid. Add the sugar to the
eggs and beat until the mixture is quite smooth. Stir in the prepared tea liquid.
Put this mixture in a bowl over a pan of boiling water and stir until the mixture
thickens. Pour into a basin to cool. Whip the cream until it forms peaks and
fold into the cool tea mixture. Freeze in the fast-freeze part of the freezer.
Otherwise use the icebox of the refrigerator set to its coldest and put the ice
cream into a container that has already been chilled.

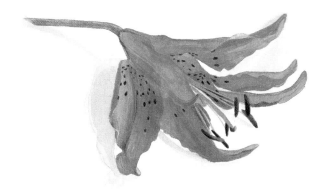

There's something attractively timeless about going out to tea. The classic menu of tea and scones is served in a variety of nostalgic settings, from the homely atmosphere of a tea shop in a small town or seaside resort to the Regency splendour of the Pump Room at Bath or the 1930s elegance of the Palm Court of London's Waldorf Hotel. So it should come as no surprise that today's tea rooms are the result of a long tradition.

The first English people to go out to tea were the customers of coffee houses in seventeenth- and early eighteenth-century London, among them that great tea-drinker, Dr Johnson. There gentlemen drank both coffee and tea, or other drinks such as chocolate, sherbet, ale, brandy and wine, in a convivial ambience rather like that of the cafés of continental Europe. And like these cafés individual coffee houses became known for the type of clientele who gathered there: Will's in Covent Garden for poets and wits; Lloyd's in the City for merchants and shipping agents; White's in St James's for politicians and aristocrats; Tom's in Devereux Court off the Strand (the birthplace of Twinings tea company) for lawyers. Sadly, these civilized centres of tea and talk gradually died out, being replaced at one extreme by rough taverns and at the other by stuffy gentlemen's clubs.

In Georgian and Regency England, Londoners went out to the Tea Gardens, having tea in the course of an afternoon or evening out with family, sweethearts and friends. But the Gardens also fell into decline, even acquiring notoriety as scenes of crime and prostitution. In the early Victorian era, though a few high-class establishments such as Gunter's in Berkeley Square served tea to the rich, the respectable middle classes had to take tea at home.

Provision for them, in the form of the tea shop, came in 1884, when the manageress of an Aerated Bread Shop near London Bridge Station persuaded the firm to let her serve tea to passers-by (who must have included office workers commuting to work from the expanding suburbs). The experiment was so successful that a chain of A.B.C.s was set up across the country, with other companies following suit. The tea shops provided inexpensive and convenient refreshment in respectable surroundings, answering especially the growing demand from a new class of working women, secretaries and typists, who had few other congenial places to go. Most famous of all were the Lyons Corner Houses, first opened in the 1890s. In their heyday they offered a glamorous setting with chandeliers, red plush chairs and a Palm Court orchestra, as well as fast and efficient service from the black-dressed, white-aproned waitresses known as 'Nippies' – all for the price (only 2d, or less than 1p) of a cup of tea.

## Scones *(makes about 12)*

8 oz/225 g self-raising flour | 1 oz/30 g caster (superfine) sugar
1/2 tsp/2.5 ml salt | 1/4 pt/142 ml milk
2 oz/60g butter or margarine | milk for glazing

Preheat oven to Gas 7/425°F/220° and lightly grease a large baking sheet (or two smaller ones). Sift the flour and salt. Rub in the fat until the mixture looks like fine breadcrumbs, then add the sugar. Mix to a soft dough with milk. Roll out the dough on a lightly floured board to 1/2 in/1 cm thickness and cut into rounds with a 1 1/2 in/4 cm cutter. Put on the baking sheet(s) and brush with milk. Bake for 10 minutes. Cool on a wire rack.

## Clotted Cream

2 quarts/2 litres Channel Island, or other rich, creamy milk

Put the milk into a large flameproof dish and leave it in a cool place for 24 hours until the cream has risen and settled on the surface. Put the bowl over a *very low* heat and heat until the bubbles rise to the surface and form a ring around the top of the pan. The time this takes depends on the depth of the pan, but it is most important that the milk does not boil. Carefully remove the pan from the heat and leave it in a cool place for another 24 hours. Then, with a slotted draining spoon, carefully skim the crusty cream from the top of the pan and put it in a bowl. Keep in the refrigerator until required.

NB The buttermilk, or skimmed milk, that remains in the dish when the cream has been removed can be used for soups, sauces and in some cake recipes.

# Maids of Honour

### MAIDS OF HONOUR *(makes about 30)*

1 lb/445 g puff pastry
½ pt/284 ml milk
4 level tbsp/60 ml white breadcrumbs (2-day-old bread is best)
4 oz/125 g butter or margarine, cut in cubes
2 level tbsp/30 ml caster (superfine) sugar
grated rind 1 lemon
2 oz/60 g ground almonds
3 eggs

Preheat the oven to Gas 6/400°F/200°C.

Roll out the pastry and cut in rounds to fit small bun or tartlet tins. Bring the milk, with the crumbs in it, to the boil, remove from the heat and leave for 5 minutes. Beat in the butter, then the sugar, rind and almonds. Although the mixture has a slight texture, make sure it has no lumps. Lastly beat in the eggs. Half fill the pastry cases with the mixture and bake for 15 minutes, or until the pastry is cooked and has shrunk from the sides of the tins and the filling is golden brown. Remove maids of honour from tin and cool on a wire rack.

### CHERRY CAKE

3 oz/90 g self-raising flour
pinch of salt
8 oz/225 g glacé cherries,
   washed and drained
6 oz/170 g butter or margarine
6 oz/170 g caster (superfine) sugar
3 eggs, beaten
3 oz/90 g ground almonds

Preheat oven to gas 3/170°C/325°F. Grease a 7 in/18 cm cake tin and line with greaseproof paper. Sieve flour and salt together. Cut cherries in half and mix them together with a little of the flour to prevent them sinking to the base of the cake when cooking. Cream butter and sugar together until they are pale and creamy. Add the beaten eggs a little at a time, adding two tablespoons of flour after half the egg has been used to keep the mixture stiff. Fold in remaining flour, cherries and ground almonds. Turn mixture into tin and bake for 1¼ hours, or until a skewer inserted into cake comes out clean.

In winter it's dark by tea-time. The air may be chilly outdoors, but inside there's a fire burning, hot tea, crumpets or pikelets to be toasted by the hearth. In this cosy setting, tea would perhaps taste best from traditional blue and white china. One of the earliest patterns in Staffordshire blue-and-white ware was Willow Pattern, introduced by Thomas Turner at Caughley in the 1780s. Though the individual motifs are typical of Chinese porcelain, this particular combination appears to be a purely British invention. The commonest form of the pattern has a romantic legend attached to it, which has been told to generations of British children to while away long winter evenings.

The story reads clockwise round the plate. It begins in a grand, two-storey mansion (we know it is a mansion, because, in China, only a rich man's home would have more than one floor). An old mandarin lived there with his one daughter, Koong-se, who passed her days in almost complete seclusion, strolling among the flowering trees and peonies of the beautiful garden. One day a young and impoverished poet called Chang, employed as a clerk in the service of the mandarin, caught sight of her. They fell in love and arranged to meet clandestinely in the twilight. Inevitably (as in all such stories), when the mandarin came to know of this, he banned Chang from his land. As for Koong-se, he had a wooden fence built around the garden to imprison her until he could arrange her marriage to a more eligible husband, a rich, powerful and ageing duke. The marriage was to take place in the spring when the peach tree came into flower.

Winter came to an end. The willow of early spring came out. Koong-se looked down the river with longing, wondering what had become of her lover. One day, a coconut shell fitted with a tiny sail floated to her on the water, carrying a poem from Chang. She answered by the same method, and began to hope. But inexorably, the peach tree began to bud.

Wedding festivities had already begun when Chang at last secretly re-entered the mandarin's house. Swiftly the lovers fled, across the river and out of the garden, Koong-se first, Chang behind her, clutching a box of precious jewels brought as a wedding gift by the bridegroom she had never met. On to the bridge after them ran the old mandarin, carrying, some say, a whip in his hand.

The lovers took refuge briefly with Koong-se's old servant in a simple house on the other side of the bridge. Soldiers sent out by the disgraced father and bridegroom were soon on their trail, however, and Chang and Koong-se made a dramatic escape by boat down the flood-swollen river. Eventually they came to a small island where they built a house, cultivated the land and planted trees. For some years they lived there blissfully until the duke at last had his revenge. His men killed Chang, and Koong-se, inconsolable, set fire to the home they had built and died inside it.

But happily the tale does not end there. For the gods took pity on the tragic lovers and transformed them into doves, caught forever in flight on the Willow Pattern plate.

## PIKELETS *(makes 30-40)*

½ tsp/2.5 ml caster (superfine) sugar
½ oz/15 g fresh yeast
  (or half quantity of dried)
½ pt/284 ml milk, warmed

8 oz/225 g plain flour, sifted
pinch salt
1 egg, beaten

Mix the sugar and yeast together and add the milk. Leave until frothy. Put the flour and salt in a bowl, make a well in the centre and with a wooden spoon or whisk gradually incorporate the milk mixture. Then add the egg. Beat the batter well to ensure there are no lumps, cover and leave in a warm place for an hour to rise. Heat a greased griddle or heavy frying pan and drop large spoonfuls of batter on to it. When small holes appear in the surface of the batter, turn the pikelets with a spatula and cook the other side. Both sides should be a pale golden brown. Keep the pikelets warm in a folded cloth and serve hot with butter and jam or honey.

## RHUBARB AND ROSEPETAL JAM
*(makes 1¾ lb/900 g)*

1 lb/455 g rhubarb, trimmed
1 lb/455 g sugar, granulated or preserving
juice of 1 lemon
2 handfuls scented rose petals – red are best
(2 oz/60 g fresh or crystallized angelica can be used instead of rose petals)

Wipe the rhubarb and cut into small pieces. Put in a bowl and cover with the sugar, add the lemon juice and leave to stand overnight. Next day, wash and chop the rose petals, put in a preserving pan with the rhubarb and sugar and bring to the boil. Boil until setting point is reached. To test for setting, put a small amount of jam on a saucer and put in the refrigerator for a few minutes. When cool, draw your finger gently over the surface of the jam. If a skin has formed or the surface wrinkles, the jam is ready. Pour the jam into clean, warm jars, cover and label.

## Walnut Layer Cake

4 oz/125 g margarine
2 tbsp/30 ml golden (corn) syrup
2 oz/60 g soft brown sugar
2 eggs
4 oz/125 g self-raising flour, sifted
2 oz/60 g walnuts, chopped and rubbed in a cloth to remove the skins

Preheat the oven to Gas 5/375°F/190°C. Beat the margarine, syrup and sugar together until light and fluffy. Add the eggs one at a time, beating well between each addition. Fold in the flour and walnuts and mix gently until smooth. Turn the mixture into a lined and greased 7 in/18 cm square cake tin and bake for 30 minutes or until the top is firm to the touch. Turn out and cool on a wire rack. When cold, split the cake horizontally into three and sandwich together with buttercream (below). Chill for about 30 minutes before slicing.

## Buttercream

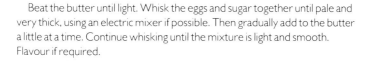

8 oz/225 g unsalted butter, softened
3 medium eggs
8 oz/225 g caster (superfine) sugar

Beat the butter until light. Whisk the eggs and sugar together until pale and very thick, using an electric mixer if possible. Then gradually add to the butter a little at a time. Continue whisking until the mixture is light and smooth. Flavour if required.

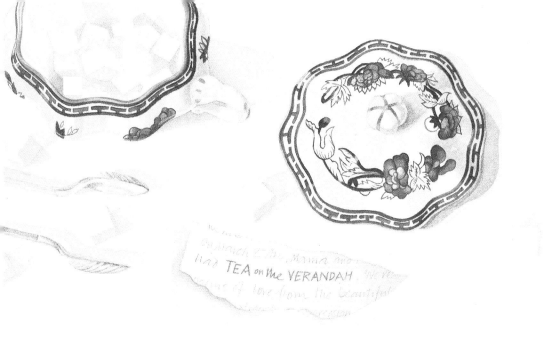

TEA on the VERANDAH

Although Indian tea is today the staple drink of the British, it was unknown in Britain before the 1830s and India did not become established as a major tea producer until the mid-nineteenth century. Before this date all the tea drunk in the West came from China,

Tea plants had been discovered growing wild in Assam in 1823 by Charles Bruce, a servant of the East India Company, but at that time the Company was unwilling to risk competition to its monopoly of the China tea trade and also considered the Indian variety of tea inferior to the Chinese. After many setbacks the cultivation of tea finally got under way on a large scale when, after the Indian Mutiny, the East India Company was abolished and the British government assumed direct rule. Planters were encouraged to settle in India and the result was a 'tea rush' in the 1860s: people from all backgrounds sailed east in the hope of making their fortune.

More than just a livelihood, tea was an integral part of the daily life of the planters and other colonial British, who became even more British abroad than at home. On hot verandahs in the Indian plains and the Burmese jungle, where only the artificial breeze of a punkah pulled by a native servant disturbed the stifling air, the British drank tea and ate the bread, buns and cakes of their northern homeland. Only rarely did local inspiration enter the menu: a pinch of spice here, a smattering of cayenne and curry powder in egg sandwiches or the subtle flavour of pistachio nuts to transform an ordinary cake into something more exotic.

## Bengal Sandwiches

1 hard-boiled egg, chopped
1 tsp/5 ml curry powder
few drops anchovy essence
a squeeze of lemon juice
cayenne pepper
salt
a little cream or butter
rye bread, thinly sliced
malt bread, thinly sliced

Pound all the ingredients, except the bread, to a smooth paste. Use as a filling for sandwiches made with rye or malt bread.

## Cold Spiced Tea

2 pt/1 litre water
3 tbsp/45 ml caster (superfine) sugar
1 vanilla pod
1 stick cinnamon
2 cloves
5-7 green cardamom pods
1 in/2.5 cm piece fresh
   ginger root
1 ½-2 tbsp/20-30 ml orange
   Pekoe tea
1-2 marigold flowers

Boil the water in a saucepan, remove from heat and add the sugar, vanilla, spices and ginger root. Leave to infuse for 15 minutes. Then add the tea. Return the saucepan to heat and simmer for 5 minutes. Strain into a jug and leave to cool. Chill. Ice can be added before serving the tea. Sprinkle marigold flowers on the tea in the jug and in the glasses.

## Anchovy and Nasturtium Sandwiches

1 oz/30 g anchovy paste
4 oz/125 g butter or margarine
nasturtium leaves
thinly sliced brown bread

Mix the anchovy paste and butter well together. Spread some of the paste on a slice of bread, place a nasturtium leaf on top, cover with another slice of bread, press together, trim off crusts and cut into small fingers or triangles.

# FEROZEPORE CAKE

| | |
|---|---|
| 16 oz/455 g plain flour | 4 oz/125 g caster (superfine) |
| pinch salt | sugar |
| 2 oz/60 g pistachio nuts | 1 tsp/5 ml orange flower water |
| 2 oz/60 g ground almonds | 1 tsp/5 ml vanilla essence |
| a few drops almond essence | 4 large eggs |
| 6 fl oz/175 ml single (light) cream | 4 yolks of large eggs |
| 10 oz/285 g unsalted butter | 4 oz/125 g chopped mixed peel |

Preheat the oven to Gas 4/350°F/180°C. Line an 8 in/20 cm round cake tin with non-stick baking paper or lightly greased greaseproof paper. Sift the flour and salt into a bowl. Put the pistachio nuts into a small saucepan, cover with cold water, bring to boil and boil for 1/2 minute. Drain, remove skins and allow to cool. Put the ground almonds, almond essence and single cream into a small basin, mix well and put aside. Cream the butter and sugar until the butter is almost white (use an electric mixer if you have one). Beat in the orange flower water and vanilla essence. Beat the yolks, one at a time, into the mixture, beating well between each addition. Add the whole eggs, one at a time, again beating well between each addition. If the mixture starts to curdle, add a spoonful or two of the flour. Gently stir the almond mixture into the creamed mixture, then carefully fold in the sifted flour, adding the nuts and peel just before the last traces of flour disappear. Turn mixture into a tin, level the surface and make a small well in the centre. Bake in the centre of the oven for 1¾ hours, or until a skewer inserted into the centre of the cake comes out clean. If liked, sprinkle a little caster sugar over the top of the cake while it is still warm. Allow the cake to cool in the tin for about 20 minutes, then remove it, peel off the paper and put on a wire rack to cool.

## Fruit Tartlets
*(makes 12)*

12 oz/340 g RICH SHORTCRUST PASTRY :
- 12 oz/340 g plain flour
- 6 oz/170 g butter
- 3 oz/90 g icing (confectioners') sugar
- 3 egg yolks
- 3 tbsp/45 ml water

PASTRY CREAM :
- 3 egg yolks
- 2 oz/60 g caster (superfine) sugar
- 1 oz/30 g plain flour
- ½ pt/284 ml milk
- 1 vanilla pod

8-16 oz/225-455 g cooked or raw fruit; many types of fruit are suitable: apple slices, apricots, pears, blueberries can be arranged before the tartlets are cooked; others, such as raspberries, strawberries, mangoes, kiwi fruit, pineapple, should be arranged once the cooked tartlets are cold.

small quantity light coloured fruit jelly

To make the pastry sift the flour into a basin. Add the butter cut in small pieces and rub into mixture. Sift in the icing sugar. Make a well in the centre, place the egg yolks and water in the well, then with a fork mix to a rough dough. Turn on to a lightly-floured working surface and knead for a few moments until smooth. Put in greaseproof paper or a polythene bag and chill in the refrigerator for about 30 minutes before using.

To make the pastry cream put the egg yolks and sugar into a bowl and work with a wooden spoon or spatula until the mixture is pale and thick. Add sifted flour. Heat the milk and vanilla pod. Remove the pod and slowly add milk to the egg mixture, stirring well. Pour into a clean pan, place over low heat, stirring until it boils. Simmer for 2-3 minutes, stirring until it thickens. Pour into a bowl and allow to cool.

Preheat the oven to Gas 7/425°F/220°C. Grease twelve 3¼ in/8 cm tartlet tins. Roll the pastry out, stamp out circles to fit the tins and line them. Spread a layer of pastry cream at the base of each tartlet, and bake for 15 minutes before or after arranging the fruit in them (depending on the fruit). When cooked remove from tins and cool on wire rack. When cold fill with fruit (if not filled before cooking) and glaze with a little warm jelly.

IRISH LINEN

TEAPOTS

In rural Britain tea traditionally meant a lavish spread on the kitchen table, not a refined drawing room affair. Here, a roughly cut chunk of crusty bread takes the place of the dainty cucumber sandwich, and the 'properness' of the tea would be judged by its wholesomeness rather than its decorum.

The old-fashioned farmhouse tea was a family meal. Workers would come in hungry from the fields, children from the village school, and all would gather in the kitchen for this, the main meal of the day. Breakfast had been eaten long ago, soon after sunrise, and lunch was most likely a cold snack of sandwiches or bread and cheese. For tea, though, there might be fresh-baked loaves, cakes and buns, creamy milk, cheese and sunny yellow butter straight from the dairy, a ham or leg of cold lamb, meat pies with golden, crumbly pastry, pickles and home-made jam.

Particularly for those who remember a country childhood, the food served at farmhouse teas represents much of the best of British cooking. Plain food it may be, but fresh from the oven nothing could taste better. There is an astonishing variety of recipes, with innumerable regional variations on a basic theme of brown, white and currant breads, buns and tea cakes, plain biscuits and spice or fruit cakes.

Farmhouse or high tea is usually eaten at about six o'clock; a light supper or snack may be taken later in the evening. In the past, a simpler afternoon tea was taken out into the fields at exceptionally busy times such as during the harvest, when everyone fit enough would work until the sun set. Typical of these working teas were those recalled by the writer H.E. Bates from his childhood in Northamptonshire: home-made brown bread with butter and plum or damson jam, dough-cake, a bread with sultanas and currants in it, caraway cake and tea in a big blue can.

A FARMHOUSE TEA

### SINGING HINNIES

8 oz/225 g plain flour
1 tsp/5 ml baking powder
pinch salt
2 oz/60 g butter
2 oz/60 g lard
3 oz/90 g currants
milk to mix

Sift the flour, baking powder and salt, rub in the fats and add the currants. Add enough milk to make a soft dough. Roll it out into a round cake about ½ in/1 cm thick, prick the top and mark it into eight sections. Cook on a hot, greased griddle for about 8 minutes on each side until golden. Serve warm, with the wedges split in half and buttered.

### GRASMERE GINGERBREAD

8 oz/225 g plain flour
4 oz/125 g pale soft brown sugar
1 tsp/5 ml ground ginger
good pinch baking powder
5 oz/140 g lightly salted butter

Preheat oven to Gas 4/350°F/180°C. Line a shallow 8 × 12 in/20 × 30cm tin with greased greaseproof paper.

Mix the dry ingredients together. Melt the butter over a low heat, and when just melted pour on to the other ingredients and mix in well. Put the mixture into the tin, pressing down to make a ¼ in/6 mm layer. Bake for 30 to 35 minutes until golden. Mark into oblong fingers, but leave to cool in tin.

A FARMHOUSE TEA

## Dundee Cake

6 oz/170 g butter or margarine
5 oz/140 g soft brown sugar
1 tsp/5 ml black treacle
finely grated rind 1 orange
finely grated rind ½ lemon
1 oz/30 g ground almonds
4 eggs, beaten
8 oz/225 g plain flour, sifted
½ tsp/2.5 ml baking powder
12 oz/340 g sultanas
1 tbsp/15 ml whisky
2 oz/60 g split blanched almonds

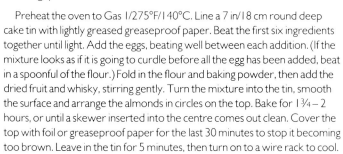

Preheat the oven to Gas 1/275°F/140°C. Line a 7 in/18 cm round deep cake tin with lightly greased greaseproof paper. Beat the first six ingredients together until light. Add the eggs, beating well between each addition. (If the mixture looks as if it is going to curdle before all the egg has been added, beat in a spoonful of the flour.) Fold in the flour and baking powder, then add the dried fruit and whisky, stirring gently. Turn the mixture into the tin, smooth the surface and arrange the almonds in circles on the top. Bake for 1 ¾ – 2 hours, or until a skewer inserted into the centre comes out clean. Cover the top with foil or greaseproof paper for the last 30 minutes to stop it becoming too brown. Leave in the tin for 5 minutes, then turn on to a wire rack to cool.

## Pitcaithly Bannock

2 oz/60 g icing (confectioners') sugar
2 oz/60 g caster (superfine) sugar
8 oz/225 g butter
8 oz/225 g plain strong white flour
4 oz/125 g cornflour (cornstarch)
2 oz/60 g flaked almonds
1 oz/30 g candied citrus peel

Preheat the oven to Gas 3/325°F/170°C. Cream sugars and butter together until smooth. Sift flours into bowl and mix in well. When you have a smooth dough add all but a few almonds, then roll out on to a round shape about 1 in/2.5 cm thick. Decorate top with remaining almonds and citrus peel, pressed in gently.

Place bannock on a greased baking sheet and bake for 40–50 minutes until it is a pale golden colour.

To the young and fashionable in the 1920s, tea belonged in the ballroom as much as in the parlour. The Bright Young Things tangoed and quickstepped through this once sedate hour of late afternoon, the tinkle of teaspoons accompanied by the strains of a jazz band or small string orchestra.

The tea dance, or *thé dansant*, first caught on in the previous decade. Restaurants, hotels and department stores had for some time been providing music at tea, but never before had the customers been invited to get up and dance between the tables. The idea perhaps derived from the Viennese custom of dancing in restaurants between courses. In Britain, in particular, its adoption marked the relaxation of strict nineteenth-century codes of conduct, according to which such Continental habits would have been considered decadent – even slightly indecent. In America the daring nature of the dances aroused controversy: in the 1910s 15 female employees of the prim *Ladies' Home Journal* were sacked for dancing the Turkey Trot – a dance in which partners clasped each other closely. Nevertheless, the tea dance continued to flourish, particularly during Prohibition. In 1919 a Ziegfeld Follies star, Bert Williams, sang his protest 'You Can't Make Your Shimmy Shake on Tea'. But the tea dancers could and did!

Free of old-fashioned inhibitions, the young generation of the early twentieth century welcomed the tea dance and each new dance craze associated with it. As well as the Turkey Trot and the Shimmy, they danced the Maxie, the suggestive Bunny Hug, the Castle Walk, the Tango, Charleston and the Black Bottom. One year everyone flocked to a Parisian-style Thé Tango; the next fashion was for exotic Hungarian teas, complete, presumably, with dashing gypsy violinists. But the real attraction of the tea

dance was the ideal opportunity it offered for men and women to meet unchaperoned at this seemingly innocent time of day, among innocent refreshments, released from their homes and offices into a setting designed to foster romance. The Palm Courts and tea rooms of hotels and large stores were extravagantly decorated in styles we now associate with Hollywood; and for a small price they allowed the mass of ordinary people to taste the glamour they saw on the movie screen. (For one dance hostess at London's famous Café de Paris, Estelle Thompson, dreams of a glamorous life did come true: discovered there, she went to Hollywood and became the film star Merle Oberon.)

In the 1930s, too, when real life was drab and depressing for many, the tea dance remained popular for the harmless pleasure and welcome touch of fantasy and elegance it brought into mundane lives.

## PINWHEEL SANDWICHES

brown loaf of bread
white loaf of bread
butter, softened
fillings such as: cooked asparagus tips, very finely chopped egg mayonnaise, crab or lobster paste, smoked cod's roe, well-flavoured ham, tongue, cream cheese and herbs.

Slice the loaves thinly lengthways, trim off the crusts and spread the bread lightly with butter. Spread with the filling. Roll up each slice from the short end, like a swiss roll (jelly roll). Chill in the refrigerator, wrapped in cling film (plastic wrap) before cutting into thin pinwheels.

## TEA KISSES

2 egg whites
4 oz/125 g caster (superfine) sugar
grated rind of half lemon

Preheat oven to Gas ½/250°F/130°C. Oil a baking tray. Whip the egg whites until stiff. Add the sugar and rind gradually, continuing to beat until the mixture is very stiff. Drop spoonfuls, or pipe stars, of the mixture on to the baking tray. Bake for 50 minutes, remove from the tray and cool on a wire rack.

## ALMOND RASPBERRY CRISPS
*(makes about 12)*

2 oz/60 g butter
2 oz/60 g caster (superfine) sugar
½ tsp/2.5 ml almond essence
2 egg whites
1 oz/30 g plain flour, sifted
1 oz/30 g ground almonds
10 fl oz/284 ml double (heavy) cream, whipped
4 tbsp/60 ml raspberry jam

Preheat oven to Gas 5/375°F/190°C. Grease two baking sheets. Put the butter and sugar in a pan and heat gently until melted. Remove from heat and add almond essence. Let cool for about 5 minutes, then fold in flour and ground almonds. Put three tablespoons of the mixture well apart on the baking sheet and spread each one to a 3 in/7.5 cm circle. Bake for 8 or 10 minutes, until brown around the edges. Remove from the oven, let cool for a few seconds, and put the next tray of three circles in the oven. With a fish slice or spatula remove the cooked crisps from the sheet and mould them gently over inverted and oiled egg cups or small glasses without stems and leave to cool. Repeat until all the mixture is used. To serve, fill each crisp with cream and top with jam.

## English Rout Biscuits
*(makes about 30)*

4 oz/125 g ground almonds
4 oz/125 g caster (superfine) sugar
few drops almond essence
2 or 3 egg yolks

Preheat oven to Gas 8/450°F/230°C. Grease and flour a baking sheet. Mix almonds and sugar and flavour with the essence. Mix to a pliable paste with the egg yolks. Do not handle too much as the mixture will become oily. Make into a variety of shapes. For example:

*Rings* Colour some of the paste pink or green and roll out quite thickly. Cut into small rings with two plain cutters of almost the same size. Brush with egg yolk and bake for about 5 minutes, until just brown at the edges. Brush with a little white icing and put four silver balls at the points of the compass.

*Chocolate sticks* Using either coloured or uncoloured paste, roll out quite thickly and cut into neat sticks. Bake for 5 minutes. When cold dip the tips in melted chocolate, then into chocolate vermicelli.

*Walnut bon-bons* Roll coloured paste into small balls. Put half a walnut on each side. Brush with egg yolk and bake for about 5 minutes.

## Brandy Cream Cups
*(makes about 10)*

8 oz/225 g plain chocolate, melted
2 tsp/10 ml icing (confectioners') sugar
1 ½ tbsp/22 ml brandy
2 oz/60 g nuts, finely chopped
10 fl oz/284 ml double (heavy) cream, whipped
10 hazelnuts, toasted or 10 strawberries, sliced

With a small spoon or spatula spread the chocolate thickly around the inside of 10 small paper cake cases placed in a bun tray (muffin pan). Chill until set hard, then peel off the paper cases. Fold icing sugar, brandy and nuts into the cream. Fill the chocolate cups with this mixture and top each with a nut or slices of strawberry.

# a Bizarre Tea

This colourful tea-table is a celebration of the work of Clarice Cliff, one of the most successful and innovative tableware designers of the Twenties and Thirties.

Born in 1899 in Tunstall, one of the Staffordshire pottery towns, Clarice Cliff was employed by A.J. Wilkinson Ltd at the Newport Pottery, Burslem, as a lithographer, transferring printed designs on to pottery before firing. Her original artistic ability was soon noticed and she was encouraged to develop her skills as a designer. In 1928 she was allowed her own small studio, decorating standard items from stock. Her first, highly unusual, designs were called 'Bizarre' and, in their geometric shapes and bright modern colours, show, perhaps, the influence of modern art, particularly Cubism, which she had seen for the first time on a recent visit to France. This first collection soon sold out, but by 1929, backed by the enthusiasm and conviction of Colley Shorter, the managing director of Wilkinson's whom Clarice later married, the whole Newport factory was given over to the production of 'Bizarre' designs and more assistants were employed as 'paintresses'. These young girls were beginners whom Clarice, now art director of the company, trained to trace simple geometric patterns outlined in black and filled in with vivid colour. The designs were painted in enamel on top of the first glaze and then re-fired to fix them permanently. This on-glaze technique allowed the use of a more brilliant range of colours than was possible with the normal under-glaze method.

Between 1929 and 1935 'Bizarre' ware reached a peak of popularity and Clarice Cliff became a celebrity. Her tableware was displayed at exhibitions and sold in all the big department stores, in whose windows the paintresses, brought to London specially by Clarice, could periodically be seen demonstrating their craft, amid much public interest. Many famous people became collectors of 'Bizarre' and the designs were constantly featured in fashion magazines.

Clarice Cliff always took a great interest in the display of her tableware – matching ceramic napkin rings, crochet table mats and embroidery patterns for tablecloths were available to complement the designs. In October 1932 there was a special exhibition at Barkers in London for which she personally arranged 30 table settings.

So it is perhaps not too fanciful to imagine that she would have approved of a 'Bizarre' tea, for which even the food is chosen to match the china, such as might have been served by a fashionable hostess of the Thirties.

## FRUIT AND MINT TEA PUNCH

1 pt/568 ml hot tea
6 oz/170 g (max) sugar
½ pt/284 ml orange juice
¼ pt/142 ml lemon juice
fruit, eg orange and lemon slices, strawberries
ice cubes
mint leaves

Strain the tea on to the sugar and add the juices. When cold, add the fruit, mint and ice cubes. Serve from a decorative jug or serving bowl.

## NASTURTIUM FLOWER SANDWICHES

white or brown bread, thinly sliced
butter or margarine, softened
cream cheese
nasturtium flowers

Spread the bread with butter or margarine, then spread half the slices with cream cheese. Set aside two or three perfect nasturtium flowers. Roughly tear the remainder in pieces and place on the cream cheese. Cover each with the remaining slices of buttered bread, pressing the bread down well. Trim off the crusts and cut into small neat fingers or triangles. Arrange on a serving plate and garnish with the remaining nasturtium flowers.

## ORANGE JUMBLES

*(makes about 36)*

4 oz/125 g caster (superfine) sugar
3 oz/90 g butter or margarine
4 oz/125 g blanched almonds, shredded
2 oz/60 g plain flour, sifted
grated rind and juice of 2 oranges
cochineal

Lightly grease two or three baking sheets and preheat the oven to Gas 4/350°F/180°C. Cream the butter and sugar until light and fluffy. Add the almonds, flour, orange rind and strain in the juice. Add just enough cochineal to colour the mixture a pale pink. Mix well and drop S-shaped spoonfuls of the mixture on to the prepared baking sheets, allowing room for each one to spread. Bake for 15 minutes until the edges are crisp.

## BIZARRE CAKE

6 oz/170 g butter
  or margarine
6 oz/170 g caster (superfine) sugar
3 large eggs
5 oz/140 g self-raising flour, sifted
4 oz/125 g plain flour, sifted
pinch salt
grated rind and juice of ½ lemon
orange food colouring

APRICOT GLAZE:
8 oz/225 g apricot jam
3 tbsp/45 ml water
lemon juice
ROYAL ICING:
  see opposite
yellow, orange, red
  and black food colourings

Grease two 6 in/15 cm round cake tins and line with greased greaseproof paper. Preheat the oven to Gas 3/325°F/170°C. Beat the butter until soft, add the sugar and cream until light and fluffy. Add the eggs one at a time, beating well between each addition. Fold in the flours and salt alternately with the strained lemon juice and rind. Put half the mixture in one of the prepared tins. Add enough colouring to the remaining mixture to make it look really orange. Mix well and turn into the remaining tin. Bake the cakes for 1 hour, until a skewer inserted into the middle come out clean. Leave the cakes in the tins for 10 minutes, then turn out, remove the paper and put on wire racks.

While the cakes are baking prepare two circular templates of thick card, one 2 in/5 cm in diameter and the other 4 in/10 cm. Also make the apricot glaze by putting the water and jam in a small pan and heating gently until the jam is dissolved. Add a little lemon juice. Sieve, return to the rinsed pan, bring to the boil and simmer until syrupy.

When the cakes are cold, split each one in half horizontally. Insert a skewer into the middle of the smallest template and insert the skewer into the middle of one of the divided cakes. Then, with a very sharp thin-bladed knife, cut around the edge of the template vertically into the cake, keeping the edge as neat as possible. Repeat the process with the other template. Then do the same with the other three rounds of cake, so that you have four central 2 in/5 cm discs, four rings 4 in/10 cm wide and four rings 6 in/15 cm wide, half of which will be bright orange.

Warm the apricot glaze and with a pastry brush spread a thin layer of glaze around the sides of a 2 in/5 cm orange disc of cake and put it in the centre of a serving plate. Spread glaze around the inside of a 4 in/10 cm ring of plain cake and place it carefully around the orange cake on the plate. Then put a 6 in/15 cm ring of orange cake around this. Spread glaze over the whole of the surface before adding the second layer, alternating the colours with the bottom layer to make a check effect, ie have a plain central disc and outer ring. Do this for the remaining two layers, until all the pieces of cake have been used.

To ice the cake, first cover the whole surface with glaze. Colour half the icing yellow and cover the cake with a layer of this. If the icing is thin and runny allow the first coat to dry completely, then add another layer. If you need to add a second layer, keep the bowl of royal icing covered with a damp cloth. When the cake is covered with the basic icing, divide the remaining icing into three smaller bowls – one amount of icing being smaller than the other two. Colour this one orange and the other two black and red. Using a fairly fine round icing nozzle, pipe the 'sunrise' outline on top and side of the cake in black, as in the illustration. Clean the nozzle and bag and pipe out the orange part of the decoration; repeat with the red icing. The red sunrays can be spread out with the blade of a knife dipped in hot water.

## ROYAL ICING (FROSTING)

1 lb/455 g icing (confectioners') sugar, sifted
2 egg whites
1 tsp/5 ml lemon juice

Put the egg whites in a large pudding basin and whisk until frothy. Gradually beat in half the icing sugar with a wooden spoon or spatula. Add half the remaining icing sugar and the lemon juice and beat until white, smooth and glossy. Then add the remaining icing sugar and beat until the icing will stand in soft peaks. Add any food colouring that the recipe requires. If time, cover bowl with a damp cloth to allow any air bubbles to rise to surface and burst before using. Otherwise use icing immediately and prick any air bubbles before icing sets to ensure it is smooth.

A Picnic Tea

In continental Europe, the idea of the picnic has ancient, faintly bacchanalian associations: the decadent *déjeuner sur l'herbe* of free-flowing wine, ripe cheeses and abundant fruit. The French call it a *pique-nique*. The British have borrowed the word but made their own peculiarly Anglo-Saxon interpretation of the custom to encompass every kind of social occasion from the most elegant feast to the humblest impromptu outing.

While to the lucky few it might mean champagne and smoked salmon served on damask and porcelain on the lawns of Ascot or Glyndebourne, to the average day-tripper it's more likely to come down to soggy sandwiches and lukewarm tea in a damp field or on a windy beach.

But an enjoyable picnic tea can and should avoid both extremes. Extravagant hampers are unnecessary. The food is easily portable in cake tins or plastic boxes and sandwiches and cake wrapped in foil will stay fresh. A greater problem is the tea itself. As connoisseurs know, a good brew can never be produced from a vacuum flask: if made in advance it will be stewed; if made on the spot, the water from the flask will not be hot enough. Stylish picnickers of the nineteenth century had one solution: they took a silver tea kettle and spirit lamp, like those used in the drawing room, with them – along with all the other teatime paraphernalia and, of course, the servants to carry it all! A simpler alternative, not however always acceptable in the British climate, would be to take iced tea, kept cool in the vacuum flask.

For however grand the occasion or careful the preparations, the success of any alfresco meal will ultimately depend on the weather. A verse by Sir John Betjeman, ever the truthful observer of his countrymen's habits, describes what is all too often the typical British picnic at a seaside resort:

On Paignton sands Hawaiian bands
Play tunes across the sea
Like 'Home Sweet Home'; above the foam
The Kegans call to me
As once again the Devon rain
Upsets their picnic tea.

## Neapolitan Sandwiches

brown or white bread, thinly sliced
butter
fillings of different colours, eg tomato, pâté, watercress, egg

Butter two slices of bread on one side only, the remainder on both sides. Place the unbuttered side of one slice on a breadboard or working-surface. Spread the buttered side with one of the fillings, cover with a slice of bread and press it well down. Build up a 'loaf' alternating the fillings to give a colourful effect. Cover the final layer of filling with the buttered side of the remaining slice of bread that was buttered on only one side. Cut off the crusts and wrap the 'loaf' tightly in foil or clingfilm and put in the refrigerator overnight with something heavy on top. Unwrap the 'loaf' and slice thinly across the layers of fillings. Cut each slice into triangles to serve.

NB Make sure that the weight covers the 'loaf' evenly otherwise it will be difficult to slice and look messy.

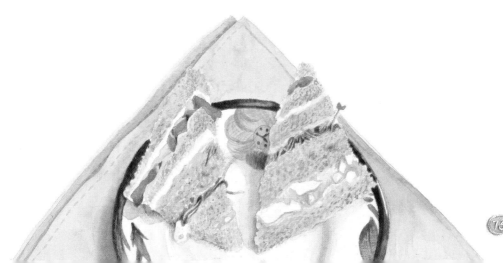

## FLORENTINES
*(makes about 30)*

1 ½ oz/45 g butter or margarine
4 fl oz/125 ml double (heavy) cream
4 oz/125 g caster (superfine) sugar
1 oz/30 g glacé cherries, rinsed in hot water, dried and quartered
7 oz/200 g blanched almonds, 5 oz/150 g finely chopped, the rest slivered
3½ oz/100 g crystallized orange peel, finely chopped
2 oz/60 g flour
8 oz/225 g plain chocolate, broken in small pieces

Preheat the oven to Gas 4/350°/180°C. Grease and lightly flour several baking sheets.

Put the butter, cream and sugar in a saucepan and bring slowly to the boil. Remove from the heat and stir in the cherries, almonds, peel and flour. Drop teaspoonfuls of the mixture on the prepared baking sheets, allowing plenty of room for the florentines to spread, and flatten each portion of the mixture with a wet fork. Bake for 5 to 6 minutes. Remove from the oven and with a 3 in/7.5 cm plain round biscuit cutter, pull in the edges of each biscuit. Return to the oven and bake for a further 5 to 6 minutes or until browned at the edges. Cool slightly on the baking sheets, then lift off with a spatula or sharp knife and put on a wire rack until cold.

Melt the chocolate in a bowl over a pan of hot water. Stir with a wooden spoon until smooth and thick. Spread the smooth side of the biscuits with chocolate and, when almost set, mark with wavy lines using a cake decorating comb or the blade of a serrated knife.

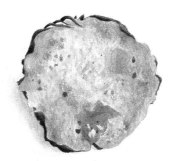

## Cider Cake

2 eggs
4 oz/125 g butter or margarine
4 oz/125 g caster (superfine) sugar
8 oz/225 g plain flour, sifted
1 tsp/5 ml baking powder
good pinch grated nutmeg
5 fl oz/142 ml cider
14 oz/400 g dessert apples (peeled weight) peeled,
    cored and cut in large segments
a little extra cider

Preheat the oven to Gas 5/375°C/190°C. Line a 9 in/23 cm diameter cake tin with a loose base with greased greaseproof paper.

Beat the eggs until thick in a basin over a pan of warm water. Cream the fat and sugar until pale and fluffy. Gradually fold in the eggs. Fold in the flour, baking powder and nutmeg and add the cider. Spoon the mixture into the tin, arrange the apple segments on the top and brush them very lightly with the extra cider to stop them drying out during the baking. Bake for 1 hour, or until a skewer put into the centre comes out clean. Cool in tin for 10 minutes and then remove and cool on a wire rack.

## Iced Tea

1 oz/30 g tea leaves                    sprig of mint
1 pt/568 ml cold water                  ice cubes
slice of lemon

Put the tea leaves in the water and leave overnight. Strain into a vacuum flask. Add ice cubes, lemon or mint shortly before serving.

For a small child today, a tea party is a magical occasion: jellies glistening like jewels, a cake iced in rainbow colours, a hush as candles are blown out and a wish is made. A look at the past, however, reveals the tea party in many other forms, from Victorian 'At Homes' for smart society in the drawing room, to the imaginary party of the Mad Hatter and his motley collection of guests. The most famous 'tea party' recorded was quite another affair. It took place in Boston harbour on December 16, 1773. No invitations were issued. It was not a celebration but a demonstration, and it marked the beginning of the American Revolution.

In 1765, the British government decided, without the consent of local American Assemblies, to tax tea imports into its American colonies. The tax was small, only 3d a pound (the British themselves had to pay much more) but the American colonists objected on principle. Many boycotted tea from England, others smuggled it in on Dutch ships, and some turned to local substitutes, so-called Liberty Teas concocted of the wild flowers, loosestrife and other plants.

The last straw came in 1773, when Parliament in London, in a heavy-handed attempt to make up for losses due to smuggling, gave the British East India Company a complete monopoly over tea imports into North America. The reaction across the Atlantic was furious. When the next three British tea ships docked in Boston, a group of American patriots, supposedly disguised as Red Indians and carrying tomahawks, descended on the ships. They smashed open all the tea chests on board and emptied their contents, valued at £10,000, into the briny water.

The Boston Tea Party may be remembered mainly for its ironic name now that the passions which caused it have faded. But the tea parties of childhood live on in the imagination, even into adult life. This wonderfully colourful table, with its amusing party sandwiches, fantastically decorated cake and intriguing little presents would surely be the setting for the most memorable tea party ever.

## Orange Sunrise

orange juice                              grenadine syrup

Pour orange juice into a glass or jug and slowly pour in some grenadine. The grenadine will sink to the bottom to produce the sunrise effect.

## Party Sandwiches

brown bread and butter
white bread and butter
FILLINGS:
peanut butter,
jam, chocolate spread,
egg mayonnaise, ham,
cheese, cream cheese,
cheese and chutney, etc.

Make sandwiches as described on page 17, then cut into fancy shapes with pastry cutters or a very sharp, fine-bladed vegetable knife – the simpler the shape the more effective it will look. Decorate savoury sandwiches as faces, using thin slices of carrot for eyes (with a blob of tomato purée in the middle), a cucumber triangle for the nose and a thin tomato segment for the mouth. (Do not make these decorations too large, or the whole sandwich will collapse messily.) The decorations can be stuck on with dabs of mayonnaise or cream cheese. Sweet sandwiches can be decorated with hundreds and thousands, silver balls, mimosa balls or chopped nuts. Spread the top of the sandwich thinly with thinned apricot jam or margarine and press the decorations firmly in place.

79

## Brandy Mop Curls *(makes about 25)*

4 oz/125 g butter
4 oz/125 g golden (corn) syrup
4 oz/125 g granulated sugar
4 oz/125 g flour

2 tsp/10 ml ground ginger
1 tsp/5 ml lemon juice
1 tbsp/15 ml brandy
pinch nutmeg

Preheat the oven to Gas 3/325°F/170°C. Line at least two baking sheets with lightly greased greaseproof paper or non-stick baking paper. Melt the butter, syrup and sugar together in a saucepan over a low heat, stirring. Remove from the heat and add the rest of the ingredients. (The mixture should be warm but not hot.) Put 6 teaspoonfuls of the mixture on one of the baking sheets with plenty of space between them as the mixture spreads. Bake for 8 to 10 minutes, or until golden brown, lacy and set. When ready, take out the first tray and put in the second. While those brandy mop curls are cooking, remove the first ones from the greaseproof paper with a spatula and shape around the handle of a wooden spoon or a rolling pin, working quickly before they harden. Slide off when shaped and allow to cool on a wire rack. Store in an airtight tin. Fill with whipped cream or soft brandy butter before serving.

## Jelly Oranges

4 oranges per packet of jelly (jello)      jelly (jello)

Cut oranges in half and scoop out the flesh. Make up jelly following instructions, but a little stronger than usual. Pour jelly mixture into orange halves and put in refrigerator to set. Serve as they are, so they can be eaten with a teaspoon, or cut each in half again for eating in the fingers.

## Party Parcel Cake

8 oz/225 g butter or margarine
8 oz/225 g caster (superfine) sugar
2 tbsp/30 ml cocoa powder
4 eggs
8 oz/225 self-raising flour
APRICOT GLAZE:
see page 68
ROYAL ICING (FROSTING):
2 lb/900 g icing
   (confectioners') sugar
4 egg whites
4 tbsp/60 ml lemon juice
pink, orange, yellow and green
   food colouring
(for method see page 69)

CHOCOLATE AND YOGHURT
FILLING:
4 oz/125 g melted
   plain (unsweetened) chocolate
5 fl oz/142 g carton thick Greek
   yoghurt or sour cream
DECORATIONS:
packet liquorice allsorts
   (mixed coloured sweets)
tube of Smarties (M&Ms)
5 chocolate marshmallows
6 chocolate finger biscuits
2 mini jam swiss rolls
4 Jammy Dodger biscuits
   (biscuits with jam centres)

Preheat the oven to Gas 4/350°C/180°. Grease two sponge cake tins, one round one 6 in/15 cm in diameter, the other a hexagonal one 6 in/15 cm across. Line the bases with lightly greased greaseproof paper. Cream the butter and sugar until pale. Lightly whisk the eggs and add a little at a time to the creamed mixture, beating well. Sift the flour and cocoa together, then fold gently into the creamed mixture. The mixture should still drop easily off a spoon. If it doesn't, add a tablespoon (15 ml) or two of hot water. Divide mixture between the two cake tins and bake in centre of oven for 30 to 35 minutes, or until centres are springy. Peel off the base papers and allow to cool on a wire rack.

Meanwhile make chocolate and yoghurt filling by combining cooled melted chocolate and yoghurt together thoroughly. (It may seem runny but will harden when spread.) Also make apricot glaze and royal icing. Make up the latter in two batches, using 1 lb/455 g icing sugar for each. Cover the bowls with a damp cloth until needed.

*To decorate the cakes*

Start with the hexagonal cake (which will be on top). Turn cake upside down to give a flat surface, then split it in half horizontally. Fill with chocolate and yoghurt filling. Replace top and put cake on a revolving cake stand or on a plate on an upturned pudding basin. Take one of the bowls of royal icing and put half the icing in another bowl. Colour one lot of icing pink, the other yellow. Cover cake with a thin layer of glaze and then with a thick layer of pink icing. Decorate top with 4 marshmallows and halved orange liquorice allsorts and sides with yellow allsorts as in picture. Leave until icing is dry. Divide remaining bowl of white icing into 4 small bowls. Add pink, green or orange to 3 bowls and leave the other white. Using a piping bag with a fine nozzle pipe round marshmallows and pipe a zigzag line on the sides. Place chocolate fingers round lower edge of cake and decorate with spots of icing. Leave to dry. Cut mini swiss rolls in half and cover with orange icing. Leave to set. Stick swiss roll halves to marshmallows with apricot glaze then put a black allsort on each. Finish decorating with coloured icing and Smarties as in illustration.

To decorate the round cake, turn upside down, split in half and fill, then put on a cake stand or plate on an upturned basin and cover with a thin layer of glaze. Cover thickly with yellow icing and place 4 allsorts on top. When icing is dry put cake on a thin round cake board 8 in/20 cm in diameter, then replace on turntable. Decorate with zigzags, filled in with pink and orange icing. Cover cakeboard with white icing. Finish decorating with allsorts, piped icing Smarties and halved Jammy Dodger biscuits as in the picture or as you choose.

*To assemble the cake*

Using glaze as 'glue' stick more allsorts on top of those on round cake to make little pillars and a marshmallow in the centre. Put 4 cake pillars on the table, place round cake on top and hexagonal cake on allsorts pillars. Arrange small presents underneath with ribbons reaching each child's plate.

Tea as a meal inevitably has nostalgic associations, explored on other pages. It evokes Edwardian formality, cosy nurseries, old-fashioned teashops, the bygone days of the Raj ...

But here is a plea for the revival of teatime as a social institution, with ideas for a Thoroughly Modern Tea. Not many people can stop work at four or five for more than a quick cup of tea, so why not hold a party a little later – say at 6 or 6.30, so that it becomes more like a cocktail party? Too early for dinner, this is just the time when people need a little sustenance; and tea as a drink is both better for reviving flagging spirits than a gin and tonic and a safer start to an evening out.

This menu would also be ideal as a pre-theatre snack or as a light late-night nibble – tea is too good to be kept just for teatime.

The black and white tea is suitably sophisticated – savoury sandwiches and canapés to stimulate the appetite and a spectacular marbled cake almost too elegant to eat are served on dramatic modern black and white china. Of course, such a chic repast requires some effort from the guests, so if you can persuade them all to dress in black and white so much the better!

You are invited to a Black and White Tea

## CAVIARE OPEN SANDWICHES

black rye and white bread, thinly sliced
sour cream
black caviare or lumpfish roe

Using a small heart-shaped pastry cutter, stamp shapes out of the unbuttered bread. In the centre of each heart put a dab of sour cream and on this a small pile of caviare.

*NB* It is important that these sandwiches are small – no larger than one polite mouthful.

## LIQUORICE PINWHEEL BISCUITS
*(makes about 24)*

6 oz/170 g plain flour
½ tsp/2·5 ml baking powder
pinch salt
3 oz/90 g margarine
3 oz/90 g caster (superfine) sugar
vanilla essence
milk
black liquorice-flavour colouring

Sieve together the flour, baking powder and salt. Cream the fat and sugar until very pale. Fold in the flour, a few drops of vanilla essence and sufficient milk to make a stiff paste. Divide the mixture in half, and blend enough liquorice colouring into one half to make the mixture black. Roll out both halves very thinly into equal-sized pieces. Place the black one on top of the white, then roll up very tightly, like a Swiss roll (jelly roll), and allow to rest in a cool place for 30 minutes to become firm. Preheat the oven to Gas 3/325°F/170°C. Grease a baking sheet. Cut the roll into slices about ¼ in/5 mm thick, put on the baking sheet and bake for 15 to 20 minutes or until very pale golden. Remove from oven and allow to cool for a few moments on the tray before transferring to a wire rack. Dust with caster sugar before serving if wished.

## SAVOURY STAR
## BISCUITS WITH CAVIARE
*(makes about 40)*

2 oz/60 g butter
¼ pt/142 ml milk
generous pinch of salt
1 oz/30 g fresh yeast or
1 tbsp/15 ml dried yeast mixed with
a little sugar in hot water and
allowed to stand for 10 minutes
12 oz/340 g plain flour, sifted
sour cream
black caviare or lumpfish roe

Put the butter and milk into a small pan and stir over a low heat until the butter has melted. Remove from the heat and when the mixture is just tepid add the salt and yeast. Leave to stand for 10 minutes or until the yeast foams. Mix the flour in thoroughly; knead the mixture well, put in a bowl, cover with a damp cloth and leave in a warm place for 15 minutes.

Roll the dough out thinly into a neat rectangle, fold one end into the centre and then fold the other end over the top. Turn the dough 90°, so that a folded edge is not towards you. Roll out into another rectangle, fold and turn as before. Repeat the process 7 times. Preheat the oven to Gas 4/350°/180°C. Roll the dough out to ¼ in/5 mm thick and stamp out with a small star-shaped cutter. Place on oiled baking sheets, prick well with a fork and bake for 20 minutes or until lightly browned. Remove from the oven and allow to stand for a few moments before putting on a wire rack to cool.

When cold put a small dab of sour cream in the centre of each biscuit and on this a small pile of caviare.

## MARBLE CAKE

4 oz/125 g butter or margarine
6 oz/170 g caster (superfine) sugar
1 tsp/5 ml vanilla essence
2 eggs
8 oz/225 g self-raising flour, sifted
pinch salt
3-4 tbsp/45-60 ml milk
1 tsp/5 ml black food colouring
10 oz/285 g icing (confectioners') sugar, sifted
black colouring
hot water

Preheat the oven to Gas 4/350°/180°C and grease a 7 in/18 cm cake tin.
Cream the butter and sugar until fluffy. Beat in the vanilla essence and then the
eggs. Fold in the flour and salt alternately with the milk. Put half the mixture into
another bowl and add the black colouring. Mix in well. Put alternate spoonfuls of the
mixtures into the baking tin, then cut through and swirl the mixture a few times with a knife.
Bake for 50 minutes to 1 hour, or until a knife inserted into the middle of the cake comes
out clean. Remove from tin and cool on wire rack.

Put 8 oz/225 g of the icing sugar into a bowl, add hot water, a few tablespoons
at a time, and mix in well before adding more to get the right consistency.
When it is a good thick coating consistency pour over the middle of
the cake and spread it with a knife blade dipped in hot water. Put
the remaining 2 oz/60 g of icing sugar in a small bowl, add the
black colouring and a little hot water. Put a fine round icing
nozzle into an icing bag and fill with the black icing.
Then, working quickly before the icing on the
cake has set, pipe swirls of black icing over the
top and sides of the cake. The two icings
will merge because they are the same
consistency. To make larger areas
of black pipe the lines very
close together and spread
out with a hot knife
blade if necessary.

Tea in bed is a special treat – a luxury that most people don't often have time for. So it's worth taking a little trouble to make the most of it – with home-made bread and jam and freshly brewed tea on a prettily laid tray. Then you can relax in total self-indulgence with the papers and the post (in this ideal scenario the postman will have brought not bills but a longed-for letter from your distant loved one). Of course, if your loved one were there to bring you tea, it would be even better...

## SCOFA BREAD

9 oz/250 g wholewheat flour
1 tsp/5 ml baking powder
1 tsp/5 ml bicarbonate of soda
pinch sea salt
½ level tsp/2.5 ml raw brown sugar
¼ oz/10 g butter
¼ pt/142 ml sour milk

Preheat the oven to Gas 6/400°F/200°C. Mix dry ingredients in a large bowl, rub in the butter. Slightly warm the milk and add to the other ingredients to form a soft dough. Knead quickly and lightly until smooth. Shape into a small round, flat loaf. Mark a cross on the top with a sharp knife. Dust with flour. Place on a baking sheet and bake immediately in the centre of the oven for 30 minutes, until golden brown on top. Cool on a wire rack. When cold the loaf can be broken into quarters.

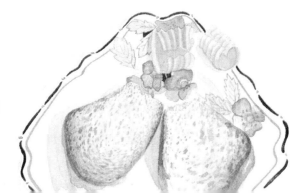

## BLACKBERRY, ELDERBERRY AND APPLE JAM

1 lb/455 g elderberries
1 lb/455 g blackberries
1 lb/455 g apples
water
juice 1 lemon
3 lb/1.3 kg granulated or preserving sugar

   Strip elderberries from stalks with a fork, removing any bad ones. Pick over blackberries, discarding bad ones. Peel, core and chop the apples to the size of the blackberries. Put barely ½ in/1 cm water in the bottom of a large pan. Add fruit, cover pan and gently simmer the fruit until soft. When soft add the lemon juice and sugar. Stir over a low heat until the sugar has dissolved. Then bring to boil and boil fast until setting point is reached. Pot the jam into clean warm jars, cover with waxed discs, wax side down, and leave to cool. When quite cold put on jam pot covers and label.

# Credits

Almost every page of this book has been enriched by people kindly lending me their treasured teaware. I would like to thank the long list of people who entrusted me with their china, silver, toys and teddies. Many of the recipes in the book were cooked by Sandy Garfield, who saved me hours in a steamy kitchen. I hope she knows how indebted I am to her for her patience. I owe a great deal to Gabrielle and Danny for the hours we spent together arranging the text, and to Lorraine for taking this on. Little did we both know ... Thank you to all the dear friends who have encouraged me through thick and thin. And to David in Haneviim where it all began.

COVER: Crown Derby teapot lent by Sue Wilde, Kew Tea Rooms, Richmond, Surrey. Tablecloth lent by Marie Jones, Georgian Galleries, Camden Passage, London N1. Crown Derby tea knife from Harrods.

TITLE PAGE: Tea-table teapot by J and G Morten from The Tea House, Neal Street, London WC2.

FOREWORD: Elephant teapot lent by Sheelagh Gilbey.

CONTENTS PAGE: Baking powder tins lent by Carrie Jaffe.

TEA INTRODUCTION: Tea caddy spoons lent by Dieter Heinen.

CHINA INTRODUCTION: 'Batavian Bamboo and Peony' teacup and saucer, examples of the Nanking cargo, lent by Ian Ogilvy.

HOW TO MAKE TEA: Harlequin teapot designed by Andy and Tamsin Ceramics from The Tea House. Faun cup and saucer lent by The Prop House, Brunel Way, London W3.

A PROPER TEA: Crown Derby teaset lent by Lily and Laurence Mitchell, Gateway Arcade, Camden Passage, London N1. Silverware lent by Rosemary Hart, Gateway Arcade, Camden Passage. Crown Derby tea knives from Harrods. Table and tablecloth from author's mother.

A NURSERY TEA: Victorian high-chair and Bertie Bear china from The Nursery, 103 Bishops Road, London SW6. Shelley teapot lent by Charlotte Humphrey. Wooden train and aeroplane lent by Carrie Jaffe. Red napkin rings lent by Michael and Polly Carter-Graham-Smith. Toy teaset and antique figures lent by Sally Buckingham and Sally-Anne Walker. Teddies lent by Coral Johnson, Rosie Turner and Sally Buckingham. Tablecloths embroidered by Clifford and Edith Heap.

TEA IN THE GARDEN: 'Oceanside' Coalport teapot from Harrods. Arts and Crafts tea kettle and silverware lent by Gloria Goldsmith, Goldsmith and Perris, Stand 327, Alfie's Antique Market, Church Street, London NW8. 1920s Collingwood bone china lent by Valerie Wolstenhome and Jim Clay. Tablecloth from Laura Ashley. Sunshine from Haneviim, Tel Aviv.

OUT TO TEA: 'Fantasy' Royal Tudorware by Barker Bros Ltd from author's collection. Carltonware menu stand lent by Michael and Polly Carter-Graham-Smith. Green tablecloth from Kakki.

TEA BY THE FIRE: 'Yuan' china by Wood and Sons from Muriel Cook, Georgian Village, Camden Passage. Jam spoon lent by Julia Watson. Tablecloth from Laura Ashley.

TEA ON THE VERANDAH: 'Indian Tree Coral' by Coalport from Wedgwood. Silver-plated tazza lent by Beverley, Units 655-7, Alfie's Antique Market. Knives lent by Beth, Units 313-4, Alfie's Antique Market. Sugar tongs lent by Chrissy, Stall R11, Chenil Galleries, Kings Road, London SW3. Ferozepore cake made by Pat Alburey. Butterfly tablecloth from author's collection.

A FARMHOUSE TEA: 1930s china by Gray of Stoke-on-Trent lent by Trudy Share, Unit 834, Alfie's Antique Market. Tablecloth and napkins from Harrods.

THÉ DANSANT: Crown Derby china owned by the late Edward James, from the collection of John Jesse and Irina Laski, 160 Kensington Church Street, London W8. Pink glove from author's mother.

BIZARRE TEA: Clarice Cliff 'Bizarre' ware lent by Aldo Taramasco at Bizarre, 24 Church Street, London NW8. Knives lent by Beth, Units 313-4, Alfie's Antique Market. Sugar tongs lent by Chrissy, Chenil Galleries. Jumbles made by Sheelagh Gilbey.

PICNIC TEA: Franciscan 'Rosepetal' china from Wedgwood. Napkins from Harrods. Pink parasol lent by Alysen of The Gallery of Antique Costume and Textiles, Church Street, London NW8. Lace parasol given by David, who also laid the foundations for the teapot studio. Binoculars and picnic basket lent by Sandy and Sheelagh Johnson.

TEA PARTY: Black and White teapot designed by Andy and Tamsin Ceramics. Multi-coloured teapot, mugs and plates by Repeat, Repeat. Table napkins by Lindy Richardson and Charlie Hackett, 9 Courcy Road, London N8. Milk jug and sugar bowl by Fox, Crosse and Gold. Cushion fabrics by Collier Campbell, Liberty, Habitat and Timney Fowler.

BLACK AND WHITE TEA: Cake plate by Fornasetti from Lilian Fawcett at Themes and Variations, 231 Westbourne Grove, London W11. Column teapot, Wrought Iron milk jug and sugar bowl by Timney Fowler, 388 Kings Road, London SW3. Guitar teapot and mugs, Aztec plates by Repeat, Repeat and black-handled knife from Graham and Green, Elgin Crescent, London W11. China tea strainer from The Tea House. Napkins from Harrods.

TEA IN BED: 1920s china from The Prop House.